The Commonwealth in Arms

A Guide to Military Sites and Museums in Pennsylvania

By John B. B. Trussell

Commonwealth of Pennsylvania
Pennsylvania Historical
and Museum Commission
Harrisburg, 1987

THE PENNSYLVANIA HISTORICAL AND MUSEUM COMMISSION

VIVIAN W. PIASECKI, *Chairman*

CLARENCE D. BELL, *Senator* LEROY PATRICK
WILLIAM H. COMBS DENISE I. ROBISON
JAMES A. FISHER JANET B. ROSS
ANN N. GREENE HARDY WILLIAMS, *Senator*
HANNAH L. HENDERSON LULA M. WITHEROW
SAMUEL W. MORRIS, *Representative* James L. Wright, Jr., *Representative*

THOMAS K. GILHOOL, *ex officio*
Secretary of Education

TRUSTEES EX OFFICIO

ROBERT P. CASEY, *Governor of the Commonwealth*
DON BAILEY, *Auditor General*
G. DAVIS GREENE, JR., *State Treasurer*

ADMINISTRATIVE STAFF

BRENT D. GLASS, *Executive Director*

NANCY D. KOLB, *Assistant Executive Director*

BRENDA BARRETT, *Director*
Bureau of Historic Sites and Museums

MICHAEL J. RIPTON, *Director*
Bureau of Historical and Museum Services

HARRY E. WHIPKEY, *Director*
Bureau of Archives and History

DONNA WILLIAMS, *Director*
Bureau for Historic Preservation

EXPLANATORY NOTE

The purpose of this booklet is to provide a guide for visitors to significant sites and museums commemorating Pennsylvania's military heritage, spanning the time from the French and Indian War two decades before the American Revolution to our country's most recent conflicts.

In order to put these sites and museums into historical perspective, their descriptions are grouped chronologically according to the war to which they primarily relate. Each grouping is preceded by a brief overview of the events treated. The pages devoted to individual sites and museums focus on the topic with which each specifically deals, and include information on what is displayed, any special observances that take place on a regular basis, resources for research, administering agency, location, visiting hours, and any admission charges (these, of course, are subject to change in the future).

It should also be noted that additional sites are currently under development. One of these is Fort Mifflin, near Philadelphia, where restoration of historic buildings is in progress. Another is the museum being developed at Fort Indiantown Gap, near Annville, Pennsylvania, which when completed will portray the roles of that installation as the headquarters for directing Pennsylvania's military activities and as a mobilization and training center during World War II.

In no way do the following accounts purport to provide a substitute for an actual visit. It is hoped, however, that they may serve the dual purpose of attracting readers to see these locations for themselves, and of contributing to a greater appreciation of the place in Pennsylvania's history of the events to which these sites and museums are dedicated

Copyright © 1987 Commonwealth of Pennsylvania

ISBN 0-89271-041-1

INTRODUCTION

Pennsylvania, despite its origin as a colony founded on principles of non-violence, has a long and distinguished military tradition. That tradition derives from the services which Pennsylvanians have rendered in all of our nation's wars. It derives, also, from the fact that Pennsylvania was the scene of some of the most decisive events in American military history.

A short battle at Fort Necessity exploded into a worldwide conflict — the French and Indian War in America, and, in its global aspects, the Seven Years War, which extended not only throughout Europe but to the Indian Subcontinent as well. That war's bloody postscript, "Pontiac's Rebellion," was brought to an end at the Battle of Bushy Run. During the American Revolution, it was from a Bucks County area now called Washington's Crossing that the Americans launched their raid across the Delaware against Trenton, New Jersey, reviving hope at a time when national morale was at its lowest ebb. Later, it was on Pennsylvania soil that the battles of Brandywine and Germantown were fought; while these were tactical defeats, they played an important role in convincing France that support of the infant United States was a worthwhile cause. Valley Forge, although it involved no combat, was a victory of the spirit which, by transforming an undisciplined mass into a trained, effective army, made possible the Revolution's ultimate success. Some thirty years later, with a fleet that was Pennsylvania built, Pennsylvania based, and partly Pennsylvania manned, Commodore Oliver Hazard Perry won the Battle of Lake Erie, a major contribution to the outcome of the War of 1812. In the Civil War the Union success at Gettysburg made inevitable the eventual defeat of the Confederacy.

Pennsylvania units and individuals also played conspicuous roles in the Mexican War, the war with Spain, the Philippine Insurrection, World War I, in all the World War II operational theaters, in Korea, and in Vietnam.

Testimony to Pennsylvania's proud military history, treating both the locations and the people, is provided by a network of museums and carefully preserved and restored sites maintained by State and national government agencies and by private organizations. They represent a tribute to the achievements of the past. With that, they provide an aid to the visitor in gaining an appreciation of the vital share of Pennsylvania and Pennsylvanians in the struggles which brought our nation into being and which have preserved it against successive armed challenges to its survival and progress.

CONTENTS

Explanatory Note iii

Introduction v

I. The French and Indian War and Pontiac's Rebellion in Pennsylvania 1

    Fort LeBoeuf 3
    Fort Necessity 5
    Carlisle Barracks 7
    Fort Ligonier 9
    Fort Pitt 11
    Bushy Run Battlefield 14

II. The Revolutionary War in Pennsylvania 17

    Washington Crossing Historic Park 19
    Brandywine Battlefield 21
    Cliveden and the Battle of Germantown .23
    Valley Forge National Historical Park, and
        Valley Forge Historical Society Museum 25

III. From the Revolution to 1812 29

    Army-Navy Museum and Marine Corps Memorial Museum 29

IV. The War of 1812 and Pennsylvania 31

    The Flagship *Niagara* 33

V. Pennsylvania and the Mexican War 36

VI. The Civil War and Pennsylvania 37

    State Museum of Pennsylvania 37
    Civil War Library and Museum of the Military Order
        of the Loyal Legion 39
    Soldiers and Sailors Memorial 39
    Gettysburg National Military Park 41

VII. The Spanish-American War and the Philippine Insurrection 45

    The Cruiser *Olympia* 46

VIII. The Pennsylvania Military Museum 48

IX. Regimental Museum 50

Section I
The French and Indian War and Pontiac's Rebellion in Pennsylvania

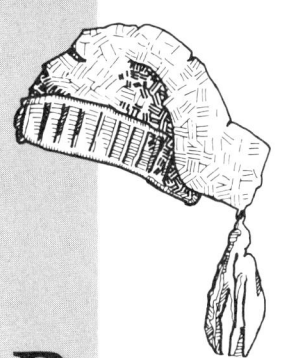

BY THE 1700s French and British rivalry, frequently marked by conflict, had existed for centuries. It was only to be expected that in America, where vast territories remained to be claimed, this rivalry would be extended through the two kingdoms' colonies.

The imperial vision of the Governor of Canada, the Marquis Duquesne, was to advance French control as far as the Gulf of Mexico. Waterways provided the only feasible routes for movement through the wilderness, but the southwestern end of Lake Erie was separated by a mere twenty overland miles from French Creek, the beginning of a network of navigable streams — the Allegheny, the Ohio, and the Mississippi — leading all the way to New Orleans and the Gulf.

Duquesne's plan began to be put into effect in 1753. By July, Fort Presqu'ile (at modern Erie, Pennsylvania) was built, with Fort LeBoeuf completed soon afterward on the banks of French Creek. Where that stream joins the Allegheny River, at Venango (now Franklin, Pennsylvania), a trading post was already in being; when garrisoned, it would be named Fort Machault. The next step would be to establish a stronghold at the Forks of the Ohio (present-day Pittsburgh), where the Monongahela meets the Allegheny to form the Ohio River.

British America, however, was equally interested in expanding into the interior of the continent, and the Virginia-based Ohio Company also claimed the territory into which the French were beginning to intrude. Consequently, on October 30, 1753, Governor Robert Dinwiddie of Virginia sent George Washington, a major in the militia, to Fort LeBoeuf with a demand that the French withdraw. Washington was only twenty-one years old, but as a surveyor, he had gained considerable knowledge of the region.

Needless to say, the French response to Dinwiddie's demand was a polite but firm refusal. By mid-January 1754 Washington had returned to Virginia. Dinwiddie promptly dispatched workmen to the strategically vital Forks of the Ohio to build a fort that would block further French expansion. He also promoted Washington and authorized him to enlist a force of Provincial troops to guard the workmen.

Before Washington could recruit his men and reach the Forks, however, French troops drove away the Virginia workmen, destroyed the fort they had begun, and built a stronghold of their own which they named Fort Duquesne. On Washington's way north he met the retreating workmen and learned what had happened, but pressed on until May 24, when he reached Great Meadows, some forty miles south of Fort Duquesne. There,

Courtesy Washington and Lee University

Col. George Washington

friendly Indians told him of a small French detachment under the Sieur de Jumonville camped only a short distance away. With the Indians, he attacked the French camp. One Frenchman escaped, however, and bore the news to Fort Duquesne. As this meant certain retaliation, Washington returned to Great Meadows and began building a defensive position which he called Fort Necessity. On July 3 the French in strength attacked him there, and after a nine-hour fight Washington surrendered.

Stung by this setback, in February 1755 the British sent a large force under Maj. Gen. Edward Braddock to capture Fort Duquesne. By July 9, having reached the Monongahela, the column was attacked and defeated (Braddock being mortally wounded) by a body of French and Indians.

Fighting had also broken out in Nova Scotia and northern New York; and on May 18, 1756, Britain formally declared war on France. This led to an expansion of the conflict across the European continent and, wherever British and French colonial interests clashed, throughout the world. In Pennsylvania, frontier settlements quickly felt the weight of French and Indian raids, and for some time the primary military effort was necessarily defense. By 1758, however, security had been sufficiently restored to permit offensive operations.

To that end, Brig. Gen. John Forbes was assigned the mission of seizing Fort Duquesne. Starting from a newly established military base at Carlisle, he built a road (the Forbes Road) westward, establishing fortified posts along the way at Fort Loudoun (near modern Loudon, Pennsylvania), Fort Bedford (now Bedford, Pennsylvania), and as a final point of departure just fifty miles from the Forks of the Ohio, Fort Ligonier (Ligonier, Pennsylvania). By November 24, Forbes's force was within one day's march of Fort Duquesne. The French garrison, seeing itself heavily outnumbered, blew up the fort and retreated toward Canada before Forbes could attack. On arriving at the ruined French stronghold the British set about building a defensive work, called Mercer's Fort; later, construction was begun on a major installation, located near but not exactly at the site of Fort Duquesne. This was named Fort Pitt.

Frontier raiding continued, but the tide had turned against the French, and a formal treaty ending the Seven Years War was signed in February, 1763.

Some of France's Indian allies, however, refused to accept this settlement. On May 9, under the leadership of the Ottawa chief Pontiac, they launched a series of violent attacks on British outposts all along the frontiers. By the end of May, Fort Pitt itself was under siege.

News of this threat started a British relief column under the command of a Swiss mercenary, Col. Henry Bouquet, marching from Carlisle. In early August it passed beyond Fort Ligonier to a point near a stream called Bushy Run. To block Bouquet's further advance the Indians abandoned their siege of Fort Pitt and laid an ambush for his force. In a hard-fought engagement on August 5 and 6 the British beat off the attack and the Indians scattered. This proved to be the final significant event of the war as far as it affected Pennsylvania, and all hostilities had ceased by the end of October.

Fort LeBoeuf

Situated so as to guarantee French access from Fort Presqu'ile at modern Erie to French Creek, the beginning of a continuous route by water to the Gulf of Mexico, Fort LeBoeuf was built in the summer and fall of 1753. From the British viewpoint, it represented a violation of British territory, and on December 11 Major George Washington arrived with a message from Governor Robert Dinwiddie of Virginia calling on the French to go back to Canada. This demand was rejected, and Washington returned to Virginia.

Hostilities began the following May, leading to the defeat of the Virginia militia under Washington (by now promoted to colonel) at Fort Necessity on July 3. The disastrous defeat of a larger British force at the Monongahela on July 9, 1755 made a general war inevitable. As hostilities continued, Fort LeBoeuf became a base for raids by the French troops and their Indian allies, but it was never directly threatened by the British. In time, with the war shifting against the French, the fort's loss became certain, and in late July 1759 it was demolished and its garrison withdrew to Canada.

Fighting continued, however. The strategic importance of Fort LeBoeuf's location prompted the British in the fall of 1760 to build and garrison a blockhouse on the site. This was occupied by a small force until June 1763, when Indians attacked. The blockhouse was burned but most of the garrison escaped.

From that time until after the American Revolution no military activity took place at this site, but the outbreak of conflict with the Indians after the Revolution again gave it significance. In June 1794, therefore, Governor Thomas Mifflin of Pennsylvania sent a militia force to build two blockhouses to secure the area. The military requirement proved to be brief, for the blockhouses were barely complete when Gen. Anthony Wayne's decisive victory at the Battle of Fallen Timbers (August 20, 1794) put an end to the Indian threat, and the garrison was soon withdrawn. By 1796 the blockhouses had been dismantled by local settlers who used the logs and stones for their own purposes.

At that time, on Gen. Anthony Wayne's orders, still another fortification was erected, near but not on the exact sites of the earlier structures. As a military installation it remained in use through the War of 1812, serving as a hospital for wounded and a stockade for prisoners of war after the Battle of Lake Erie in 1813. In subsequent years, however, it was abandoned, the land passing to private ownership. In time the surviving buildings were converted into a hotel, which was destroyed by fire in 1868.

The Fort LeBoeuf Museum, a modern building in the vicinity of the sites of the forts, offers self-conducted tours in which the visitor can view exhibits related to the history both of the fort

Fort LeBoeuf Museum

and the region's early period. These include a model of the French fort as it appeared in 1753 and of the British fort which replaced it, displays explaining the trade in beaver furs, and a treatment of the differences between the French and British approaches to colonization. One part of the museum is the Indian Room, featuring a reduced-scale model of a palisaded Indian village rendered in minute detail. A slide show provides an orientation on George Washington's 1753 visit.

In front of the museum is a statue of Washington as an officer of the Virginia Provincial troops. Also of interest and accessible to visitors are two nearby buildings, both dating from the 1820s. One is the Judson House, an example of Greek Revival architecture, furnished in period style. The other is the Eagle Hotel, typifying accommodations for travelers in the region during the early nineteenth century.

Administered by: Edinboro University of Pennsylvania for the Pennsylvania Historical and Museum Commission

Address: Edinboro University of Pennsylvania
Department of Sociology, Anthropology and Social Work
Edinboro, PA 16444
Telephone: (814) 732-2573

Location: On U.S. 19, at Waterford, PA

Visiting hours: Third Sunday of each month, March-November, 1-4 P.M.
(Closed December-February)
Guided tours for groups arranged at other times through appointment.

Admission charge: None

Fort Necessity

Fort Necessity

To block an anticipated move by the French from Canada, early in 1754 Governor Robert Dinwiddie of Virginia sent a body of workmen to build a fort at the strategically vital Forks of the Ohio. For their protection, they were followed by a force of militia under Col. George Washington. Before the British fort was completed, and well before Washington could arrive, however, a large French force appeared at the Forks, drove away the Virginia workmen, destroyed the incomplete fort, and erected a French stronghold, Fort Duquesne, in its place.

On Washington's way north he learned of the French action when he met the returning workmen, but continued his advance. By May 24 he reached a marshy area called Great Meadows. There he received word from friendly Indians that a small French force was camped a few miles to the north. With part of his troops, reinforced by the Indians, on May 28 he surprised the French camp; the French commander, the Sieur de Jumonville, and nine of his men were killed and the rest — except one who escaped to carry the news to Fort Duquesne — were captured.

Expecting reprisal, Washington returned to Great Meadows and began fortifying the position by throwing up a small stockade, which he named Fort Necessity, and digging earthworks. Early in June, reinforcements from Virginia and South Carolina brought the strength of his command to almost four hundred, but the site was unhealthful and almost a fourth of the men fell sick. Moreover, the French who appeared on July 3 numbered approximately six hundred, and they were augmented by about a hundred Indians. Fighting commenced, continuing until a heavy rain flooded the low ground and ruined the Americans' gunpowder. Outnumbered, out of ammunition, low on rations, and with a substantial number of wounded added to the sick, Washington saw no choice but to accept the French terms of surrender. On July 4 his force marched out with the honors of war to return to Virginia.

The Fort Necessity National Battlefield today features a reconstruction of the stockade, based on archeological research. The Visitors Center offers an audiovisual (slide show) orientation on the events leading up to and characterizing the battle, a diorama, artifact exhibits, mannequins displaying British and French uniforms of the period, and an illuminated map explaining the sequence of strategic events. A bookstore sells publications relating to George Washington and the French and Indian War, slides and postcards. Guided tours are provided. During the summer months living history demonstrations of uniforms, equipment and weapons are presented daily, with periodic encampments and re-enactments taking place on special occasions. For the use of researchers, a collection is maintained of some twelve hundred volumes dealing with the French and Indian War, the National Road and early transportation, and environmental education.

Nearby are Jumonville Glen, where Washington attacked the French; Mount Washington Tavern, dating from about 1827, which is maintained as a museum depicting an inn of the Old National Road; and the grave of Gen. Edward Braddock, killed during the unsuccessful British attempt to attack Fort Duquesne in July 1755.

Administered by: National Park Service, U.S. Department of the Interior

Address: Fort Necessity National Battlefield
R.D. 2, Box 528, Farmington, PA 15437
Telephone: (412) 329-5512

Location: On U.S. 40, 11 miles south of Uniontown, PA

Visiting hours: Daily, 10:30 A.M.-5 P.M. (from approximately June 15 to approximately September 1, inquire locally) (Closed New Year's, Thanksgiving, Christmas days)

Admission charge: None

Carlisle Barracks

Established in 1757 as a British Army operating base for the French and Indian War, "the Camp at Carlisle" served as the starting point the following year for Brig. Gen. John Forbes's operation which led to the British occupation of the Forks of the Ohio. In 1763, Carlisle was the assembly point for the force which, under Col. Henry Bouquet, marched to raise the siege of Fort Pitt, en route defeating the Indians at the Battle of Bushy Run, thereby ending the hostilities of Pontiac's Rebellion in Pennsylvania.

Peace led to the abandonment of the camp, but it was reopened (under the name "Washingtonburg") during the American Revolution as the Continental Army's arsenal for manufacturing and repairing weapons, and its school for artillery. Hence, only West Point is older than Carlisle Barracks as an active post of the United States Army. Like West Point, Carlisle Barracks has been used as a center for important military educational and training activities.

In the War of 1812 it was a recruit depot (basic training center) for dragoons, and from 1838 to 1861 it was the Army's Cavalry School. Burned by Confederates in 1863 during the Gettysburg campaign, it was rebuilt. From 1879 to 1918 it housed the Indian Industrial (vocational training) School, initiated under Army auspices, which became famous for its outstanding athletes. From 1920 until 1946 it was the site of the U.S. Army Medical Field Service School. Since 1951 it has been the home of the U.S. Army War College, where selected lieutenant colonels and colonels are prepared for positions of the highest military authority and responsibility. Also located at the post is the U.S. Army Military History Institute.

Hessian Powder Magazine and Museum

Upton Hall

Points of particular interest to the visitor are the Hessian Powder Magazine and Museum, built in 1777 by prisoners of war and featuring dioramas and exhibits of objects portraying the history of the post from its establishment to the present; and the Omar N. Bradley Museum, in Upton Hall, which is devoted to the life and achievements of one of America's most distinguished generals. For the researcher in military history, the U.S. Army Military History Institute offers a collection of some three hundred thousand books, over twenty thousand periodicals, and thousands of documents, photographs and personal papers relating to the U.S. Army.

Administered by: U.S. Department of the Army

Address: U.S. Army Military History Institute
Carlisle Barracks, PA 17013
Telephone: (717) 235-3434

Location: On U.S. 11 (North Hanover Street), Carlisle, PA

Visiting hours: Hessian Powder Magazine and Museum
Saturdays and Sundays, June 1-September 30, 1-4 P.M.
(Closed holidays and October 1-May 31)
Omar N. Bradley Museum
Mondays, 8 A.M.-12 NOON (Closed holidays)
Wednesdays and Fridays, 1-4:30 P.M. (Closed holidays)
U.S. Army Military History Institute
Mondays through Fridays, 8 A.M.-4:30 P.M. (Closed holidays)

Admission charge: None

Fort Ligonier

After the initial defeats at Fort Necessity in 1754 and on the Monongahela in 1755, and the concentration on defensive efforts through 1757, the British in America were able to seize the initiative and begin offensive operations in 1758. The strategic objectives were Louisburg and Quebec in Canada, Crown Point in New York; and, in Pennsylvania, Fort Duquesne.

From the base established at Carlisle, Brig. Gen. John Forbes led a column made up of British Regulars and Pennsylvania and Virginia Provincial troops westward toward the Forks of the Ohio. Most of the route led through a mountainous wilderness traversed only by streams and trails, insufficient for the baggage train required by an army of such size, so the troops built a road as they advanced, establishing fortified supply points along the way. The farthermost of these, designed as the jumping-off point for the final assault, was near the Indian village of Loyalhannon. Begun on September 3, it was named Fort Ligonier in honor of Field Marshal Sir John (later Lord) Ligonier, Commander-in-Chief of the British Army.

The French were well aware of Forbes's progress and the threat it posed. To hamper his further advance, on October 12 French and Indian forces made a major attack against Fort Ligonier. Beaten off, they made another attempt to storm the fort on November 12, but again were repulsed. Forbes then resumed his march on November 18, reaching the Forks of the Ohio on November 25 to find Fort Duquesne in ruins and its French garrison departed.

Fort Ligonier continued to be garrisoned throughout the remainder of hostilities. In July 1759 a body of French and Indians attacked the post but were driven off by cannon fire. On August 2, 1763, with Fort Pitt under siege, Fort Ligonier again became the scene of major military activity when Col. Henry Bouquet arrived with a relief column. Fearful that Fort Pitt was in dire straits, Bouquet decided that haste was imperative. To permit more rapid movement, he packed his essential supplies of flour in bags and loaded them on pack horses, moving out to win the Battle of Bushy Run that ended the significant fighting in Pennsylvania.

Three years later, Fort Ligonier was abandoned as a military installation. During the American Revolution, however, it again came into use as a base for rangers of the Pennsylvania militia and as a refuge for settlers when Indians raided. After these attacks came to an end in 1783, the fort once more was abandoned.

For the visitor today, a reconstructed fort provides a graphic picture of the bastions, palisaded walls, outer works, and buildings of the original installation. Included are such facilities as enlisted men's barracks, officers' mess and quarters, powder magazine, surgeon's office, and supply room, each of which displays life-size figures wearing uniforms of the day. A visitor-activated sound track provides explanations of the functions of the buildings in question.

At the Visitors Center and Museum an orientation film explains the historical background and significance of the fort. An illuminated map, dioramas, and displays of artifacts found during the archeological research that led to the reconstruction contribute further to understanding both of the campaign and of the site. In addition, a room furnished in formal eighteenth-century

Fort Ligonier

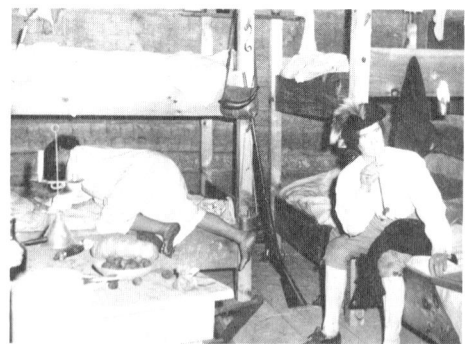
Fort Ligonier interior

style depicts the drawing room of Lord Ligonier's London house. Another period room which is maintained was removed intact from the house of Maj. Gen. Arthur St. Clair. During the French and Indian War he served as one of the fort's commanders, later resigning from the British Army to settle in the area. During the Revolution he became Pennsylvania's most senior Continental officer, and returned to military service once more to command the American army in the early stages of the Indian wars of the 1790s in the Old Northwest.

An annual event of particular interest, featuring re-enactments, encampments, and demonstrations of frontier and woodland Indian crafts and life, is called Fort Ligonier Days, a community activity held normally during the second week of October.

A gift shop offers books relating to Fort Ligonier and western Pennsylvania history, postcards, slides and souvenirs.

Administered by: Fort Ligonier Association

Address: Fort Ligonier
South Market Street
Ligonier, PA 15658
Telephone: (412) 238-9701

Location: Intersection of U.S. 30 and Pa. 711, Ligonier, PA

Visiting hours: April 1-October 31; daily, 9 A.M.-5 P.M. (Closed November 1-March 31)

Admission charge: Adult, $3.00
Children (ages 6-12), $1.50 (Group rates available by arrangement)

Fort Pitt

In an era when waterways provided the principal route for commerce and travel, the triangle of land at the point where the Monongahela and Allegheny merge to form the Ohio River was of enormous strategic importance to anyone seeking to move into the American heartland. To block such movement by the French, the British began building a fortification at that location in the winter of 1754, only to have their workmen driven away by a French force, which replaced the English works with their own stronghold, Fort Duquesne.

In the following year, Maj. Gen. Edward Braddock led a full-scale effort to capture this vital position. On July 9, 1755, however, a force from Fort Duquesne intercepted and defeated the British column. During the next three years, with the French in control of the area, Fort Duquesne became a base from which French troops and their Indian allies terrorized the frontiers of Pennsylvania and western Virginia. In 1758, however, the British were able to resume the offensive, launching attacks against strategic objectives in Canada and the northern frontier, combined with a major movement against Fort Duquesne.

That expedition, commanded by Brig. Gen. John Forbes, moved out from its base at Carlisle, building a road and erecting a series of fortified supply points as it advanced. The last of these, Fort Ligonier, was begun in early September. From there, Forbes sent Maj. James Grant with a detachment to reconnoiter. Arriving before Fort Duquesne on September 11, he impetuously attacked, only to meet a bloody repulse. Even so, neither this nor the French and Indian attacks on Fort Ligonier on October 12 and November 12 seriously deterred General Forbes. By November 24 his column was within a day's march of Fort Duquesne. With a fortification too weak and a garrison too small to withstand an attack in the strength now facing them, the French destroyed the fort and retreated northward. On Forbes's arrival the next day, he began building a temporary defensive work, Mercer's Fort. With immediate security needs met, work began on a major fortification which he named in honor of Prime Minister William Pitt.

Over the next few years, this installation was strengthened and substantially modified, in time becoming the most elaborate British fort in America. Except for sporadic marauding by Indians, however, it saw serious attack only once: beginning on May 29, 1763, as part of the widespread attack directed by Pontiac against all frontier outposts, Indians maintained a siege against Fort Pitt that continued until early August. On August 3, anticipating the arrival of Col. Henry Bouquet's relief column, many of the Indians left Fort Pitt to intercept the British. In a two-day battle at Bushy Run on August 5-6 they were defeated and scattered, and the remaining besiegers departed. With that, open conflict was ended, although sporadic raiding continued. To bring such forays to an end, in 1764 Bouquet led an expedition from Fort Pitt which pushed deep into the Ohio country and restored peace for a number of years.

During the Revolution, Fort Pitt became the headquarters of the Continental Army's Western Department. As such, it was the central coordinating point for responses to the Indian raids which resumed in 1778 and continued into 1783. With the end of the war, it became one of two storage depots

(West Point being the other) for the military supplies and equipment retained by the government. As settlers moved westward after the war, however, Indian attacks in outlying areas again became a problem. By that time, much of the earlier construction had fallen prey to weather and neglect. In 1792, therefore, still another strongpoint, Fort Fayette, was built in the area. This served as a base for the army assembling under Gen. Anthony Wayne, which then moved down the Ohio River to establish a training center at Legionville, and then to push on to win a decisive victory over the Indians at the Battle of Fallen Timbers.

Fort Fayette continued to be garrisoned through the War of 1812. Although not directly involved in combat, it was a collecting point for supplies and a training center for recruits to support military operations in the area of the Great Lakes. After the Battle of Lake Erie in 1813 it also housed prisoners of war captured in that action. At the end of he war in 1815, however, the post was inactivated and the property sold.

The only structure surviving from the British fort is one blockhouse. This was built in 1764 on Colonel Bouquet's orders to provide covering fire over the moat (which ran dry whenever the river was low, therefore offering no protection) on the Allegheny side of the ramparts. Today, a restoration of the fort's Monongahela Bastion is also maintained as a museum treating not only the historical events associated with Fort Pitt but also the development of Pittsburgh as an Indian trading post, a frontier settlement, an early transportation hub, an industrial giant, and an intellectual and cultural center.

The Fort Pitt Blockhouse contains a gift shop and some examples of antique weapons and artifacts. It is the Blockhouse itself, however, which is the center of interest, both as a relic of the original fort and as an example of the military architecture of that time.

The Fort Pitt Museum offers an orientation film on the French and Indian War and early settlement in the region, and an array of dioramas, relief maps, artifact exhibits, period rooms, uniformed models, and paintings covering the history of the Pittsburgh area, with special emphasis on the military

Fort Pitt Blockhouse

Fort Pitt Museum

Trader's cabin exhibit, Fort Pitt Museum

events affecting Fort Pitt and on the living conditions of the garrison. Rotating exhibits on a variety of subjects are also presented. A museum store features publications relating to Pennsylvania history, souvenir items, postcards, slides, pictures, and Indian craftwork.

A special event of particular interest to the visitor is the living history exhibit by a re-enactment group portraying Colonel Bouquet's Royal American Regiment. At 2 P.M. each Sunday from mid-June through Labor Day, it demonstrates the drill, field music, uniforms and equipment of the eighteenth-century British Army.

	Fort Pitt Blockhouse	**Fort Pitt Museum**
Administered by:	Fort Pitt Society, Daughters of the American Revolution	Pennsylvania Historical and Museum Commission
Address:	Fort Pitt Blockhouse Point State Park Pittsburgh, PA 15222 Telephone: (412) 471-1764	Fort Pitt Museum Point State Park Pittsburgh, PA 15222 Telephone: (412) 281-9284
Location:	Point State Park, Pittsburgh, PA	
Visiting hours:	Wednesdays through Saturdays, 10 A.M.-4 P.M. Sundays, 12 NOON-4 P.M. (Closed Mondays, Tuesdays)	Wednesdays through Saturdays, 9 A.M.-5 P.M. Sundays, 12 NOON-5 P.M. (Closed Mondays, Tuesdays and State holidays)
Admission charge:	None	Adults, $1.50 Children under 12, $.50 Senior citizens (over age 65), $1.00 Group rates, $1.00 per person

Bushy Run Battlefield

From 1760 onward, the British successively took over former French forts on the frontier, fueling growing resentment among the Indians who had been allies of the French. Officially, the French and Indian War ended by treaty in February 1763, but the Indians' rising anger erupted in May with a rapid resumption of hostilities. On May 9 the Ottawa chief Pontiac laid siege to the British garrison at Detroit. Other Indians quickly followed his lead, and forts in Ohio, Michigan, Indiana and western Pennsylvania were attacked in rapid succession, several of them falling to the Indians. Before the month was over, Fort Pitt itself was under sporadic siege.

The threat to so vital an installation demanded British action. As rapidly as possible, Col. Henry Bouquet collected

Col. Henry Bouquet

troops and supplies at Carlisle, and on July 18 he started westward on the Forbes Road at the head of 460 British Regulars together with a supply train of chartered wagons with civilian drivers. At Fort Bedford, Bouquet found the garrison so weak that he had to reinforce it with one of his companies before moving on to Fort Ligonier. After arriving there on August 2 he was joined by a company of Provincial rangers under a Maryland militiaman, Capt. Lemuel Barrett, but he also learned that for more than a month no word had got through from Fort Pitt. This alarming news emphasized the need to move on more quickly than wagons could travel. Bouquet therefore had his flour supplies transferred from barrels to bags, which were loaded on pack horses, and by the morning of August 4 the column started on the final leg of its journey.

Having learned of Bouquet's progress, a substantial part of the Indians attacking Fort Pitt had temporarily abandoned their siege to intercept him. Early in the afternoon of August 5, as the column's advance elements neared Bushy Run about twenty-five miles east of Fort Pitt, the Indians struck. Their attack was beaten off but sniping continued; and the pack train, halted on a hill about a mile to the rear, also came under fire. With the force in danger of being cut in two, Bouquet ordered the troops with him to fight their way back to the pack train.

The hill where the train had halted provided a good defensive position. The wounded were put on the rounded crest and protected by a barricade built of the flour bags. The rest of the troops manned a defensive perimeter ringing the hill partway down its slope. The eastern face, too precipitous for an enemy to approach, required no protection.

At daylight on August 6 the Indians resumed their attacks, never being able to overrun the perimeter but inflicting casualties with each assault. With

14

Imperial Oil Collection — The battle, painted by C. W. Jefferys

losses mounting and water running short, Bouquet saw that his only hope was to lure the Indians into the open where they could be shattered by volley fire.

Accordingly, he adopted a risky maneuver. On his orders, two companies fell back from the forward line as if retreating and moved out of sight below the hill. Seeing the defenses appearing to crumble, a large number of the Indians swarmed forward, moving directly in front of the two hidden companies, which struck the Indian flank with a bayonet charge. This drove them past other companies which took them under a shattering fire on their other flank. At that, the rest of the Indians also fled, the British pursuing for some distance.

That ended the battle. So far as Pennsylvania was involved, it also ended the war. Slowed by his wounded, Bouquet took up the march as soon as possible, finally reaching Fort Pitt on August 10.

Today, the visitor can take a self-guided tour to examine the area where the fighting took place and see the location of the barricade which sheltered the wounded. At the Visitors Center a museum displays a large relief map with visitor-activated electric markers and a taped narration of Bouquet's expedition, paintings depicting the action, and displays of weapons, equipment and artifacts of the period. A museum store offers relevant publications and memorabilia.

Special events include a French and

Bushy Run museum

Indian War seminar featuring a three-day encampment, a series of lectures, and equipment demonstrations during the second weekend in June; a re-enactment of the battle on the weekend nearest its anniversary (August 5-6) and a fund-raising eighteenth-century-style Thanksgiving dinner two Saturdays before Thanksgiving Day.

Administered by: Pennsylvania Historical and Museum Commission

Address: Bushy Run Battlefield
   Bushy Run Road
   Jeannette, PA 15644
   Telephone: (412) 527-5584

Location: Three miles north of Jeannette, PA on Pa. 993 between Pa. 66 and Pa. 130.

Visiting Hours: Museum
   Tuesdays through Saturdays, 9 A.M.-5 P.M.
   Sundays, 12 NOON-5 P.M.
   (Closed Mondays and State holidays except Memorial Day, Independence Day, and Labor Day)
   Park
   When Standard Time is in effect, 9 A.M.- 5 P.M.
   When Daylight Saving Time is in effect, 9 A.M.-8 P.M.

Admission Charge: Museum
   Adults (age 18-64), $1.50
   Youths (ages 6-17), $.50
   Senior citizens, $1.00
   Group rates, $1.00 per individual
   Park
   None

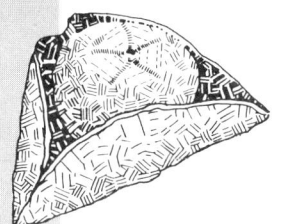

Section II

The Revolutionary War in Pennsylvania

HOSTILITIES began with the battles of Lexington and Concord, Massachusetts, on April 19, 1775. Pennsylvania troops soon joined the American forces gathered around Boston, and some of them took part in the advance into Canada that unsuccessfully sought to capture Quebec. Other Pennsylvanians were part of the operations into Canada from Fort Ticonderoga down the St. Lawrence River. Pennsylvania units also were involved in the battles of Long Island in August 1776, and Fort Washington, New York in November.

After that defeat, the center of action moved south and Pennsylvania territory itself became involved. In early December the retreat through New Jersey brought Washington's army across the Delaware and into Bucks County. It was from there, with despair sweeping through the country, that Washington carried out his master stroke, crossing the Delaware River on Christmas night to surprise the Hessian garrison of Trenton, New Jersey early the next morning, a success which he followed up early in January 1777 with a sudden raid on Princeton.

In the following summer, while a British army under Gen. John Burgoyne moved south from Lake Champlain toward the Hudson River, the British forces in New York City under Maj. Gen. William Howe boarded ship and sailed to Hampton Roads, then up the Chesapeake to land on August 24 at what is now Elkton, Maryland. Philadelphia was their objective.

Anticipating Howe's move, Washington had already marched south. On September 11 the two armies met along the Brandywine at Chadds Ford. Although the battle ended with an American retreat, the British had bought their victory at a high cost in casualties. Washington still hoped to prevent them from crossing the Schuylkill River, which lay between them and their goal. However, a northward feint by Howe sent the Americans hurrying to protect their supply base at Reading, leaving the Schuylkill fords open, and a British detachment occupied Philadelphia on September 26.

Cautiously, however, Howe kept the main part of his army on guard at Germantown, upstream from the city. Here Washington struck early on the morning of October 4. Except for misfortune, the attack almost certainly would have succeeded, but after a bloody struggle carried out in dense fog, the Americans again withdrew, this time to a position north of Philadelphia, at Whitemarsh.

Meanwhile, the easy approach to Philadelphia by way of the Delaware River, which was vital to the British as a supply route, was denied by two American strongholds, Fort Mifflin just downstream from the city and Fort Mercer, across the river in New Jersey.

On October 10 the British began a major bombardment of Fort Mifflin. Not until November 15 were the battered ruins evacuated, and Fort Mercer was held for five more days. The British followed these successes in early December by a tentative probe toward Whitemarsh. Finding the position too strong, Howe abandoned this operation, and major activities ended for the winter.

On December 19 the Americans moved into winter quarters at Valley Forge, eighteen miles west of Philadelphia. The following six months proved to be one of the severest tests the army endured during the war. Through February 1778, the men suffered severely from hunger and cold, but the later winter and spring brought a training program, designed and directed by the Prussian volunteer, Friedrich von Steuben, which for the first time developed the men into disciplined, capable soldiers. May brought the news that France had entered the war as an American ally, and it was an army in the real sense of the word which took the field on June 19 to pursue the British, who had evacuated Philadelphia and were marching through New Jersey toward Sandy Hook, where ships waited to take them back to New York.

On June 28 the Americans caught up with the British rear guard and launched an attack which brought on the Battle of Monmouth, the largest pitched battle of the war. An opportunity to inflict a decisive blow was lost; the British got away, but only to continue their retreat to New York City. From that time until the siege at Yorktown more than three years later, no significant combat between the armies took place in the Middle Atlantic area.

In Pennsylvania, however, the war took on a new face. In early July, a force of Loyalists and Indians moved down the North Branch of the Susquehanna from New York to attack the Wyoming Valley. This signaled the start of a succession of Indian raids along the frontier stretching from the Delaware Water Gap in the northeast to the southwestern regions of the State. With the Pennsylvania regiments of the Continental Army serving under Washington above New York City, the attacks in Pennsylvania had to be met as well as possible with local militia and ranger companies. In the summer of 1779, however, a force of Continentals that was massive for the time was assembled in the Wilkes-Barre area. Under Gen. John Sullivan, it advanced into the home territory of the Iroquois in upstate New York. It saw little fighting, but by destroying the Indians' crops and villages it seriously reduced their ability to continue their aggressions. Simultaneously, a smaller force under Col. Daniel Brodhead moved up the Allegheny from Fort Pitt, carrying out a similar mission.

Indian raids continued all through and beyond the end of the war, but they were on a much reduced scale. So far as conventional operations were concerned, Pennsylvania itself saw no more combat. Pennsylvania units, however, took part in the campaign in Virginia which ended at Yorktown in October 1781, and then moved south to share in the operations leading to the British evacuation of Savannah, Georgia on July 12, 1782, and of Charleston, South Carolina the following December 12. These essentially if not formally ended the war.

The crossing, painted by Emanuel Leutze

Washington Crossing Historic Park

In 1776 the succession of defeats at the battles of Long Island (August 27), White Plains (October 28), and Fort Washington (November 16) left Washington no option but to retreat to the south. The British followed closely as the Americans made their way through New Jersey, finally crossing the Delaware River into Pennsylvania in early December. At that point the pursuit halted. Washington had collected all available boats, but he could feel secure only until the river froze and ice formed a bridge for the British to cross.

Morale was extremely low. Congress had fled from Philadelphia, the soldiers' enlistments were expiring (and many had already deserted), food was in short supply, large numbers were in rags, and many were barefoot. Defeat seemed inevitable.

Desperate circumstances dictate desperate risks. Washington, whose instinct was to take the offensive whenever possible, assembled his troops near Bowman's Hill and McConkey's Ferry. Using the Durham boats that were the main cargo carriers for river traffic and such other craft as could be collected, the army crossed the Delaware on the night of December 25, assembled on the New Jersey side of the river, and in the early morning fell upon the unsuspecting Hessian garrison at Trenton. Although the victory was complete, the military impact was comparatively slight. Psychologically, however, the raid on Trenton (and the blow at Princeton which soon followed) were vitally important in restoring national confidence in the possibility of ultimate success. For that reason, it is not too much to say that the Battle of Trenton, while representing only a minor setback to British capabilities, was a major turning point in the Revolutionary War.

Washington Crossing Historic Park is now a site maintained by the Pennsylvania Historical and Museum Commission in cooperation with the Washington Crossing Park Commission. Replicas of Durham boats such as those used by the troops in the crossing are on display. The visitor may also see McConkey's Ferry Inn, where tradition says Washington and his staff dined before boarding the boats; the Thompson-Neely House, headquarters for Gen. William Alexander (Lord Stirling); the Durham Boat House, containing exhibits on Delaware River transportation; and Bowman's Hill (marked by a memorial tower), which served as an observation post during the encampment. At the Memorial Building and Visitors Center an orien-

McConkey's Ferry Inn

Thompson-Neely House

tation film is shown and a reproduction of Emanuel Leutze's painting, "Washington Crossing the Delaware," is on display. Also in the park are structures depicting early Pennsylvania life and furnishings — the Thompson Mill Barn, the Thompson Grist Mill, and the Mahlon K. Taylor House, a restored residence of the nineteenth century. One hundred acres are devoted to a wildflower preserve, with a headquarters housing a wildlife observatory and exhibits and a birdlife collection.

An annual event of particular interest is the re-enactment of the crossing, which is staged each Christmas Day. For researchers, a collection of books and other documents provides information on the campaign and the region. Also maintained is a museum store, where pertinent publications and other items may be purchased.

Administerd by: Pennsylvania Historical and Museum Commission, in cooperation with the Washington Crossing Park Commission

Address: Washington Crossing Historic Park
P.O. Box 103
Washington Crossing, PA 18977
Telephone: (215) 493-4076

Location: Washington Crossing, PA

Visiting hours: Mondays through Saturdays, 9 A.M.-5 P.M.
Sundays, 12 NOON-5 P.M.
(Closed New Year's, Columbus, and Thanksgiving days)

Admission charge: Historic buildings (single charge covers all)
Adults, $1.50
Youths (ages 6-17), $.50
Senior citizens (65 and over) and (by reservation) tour group members, $1.00
Bowman's Hill and Tower
Adults, $2.00
Children under 12, $.50
Senior citizens (65 and over), $1.50
Members of school and Scout groups (by reservation):
Ages 12 and over, $1.00; under 12, $.50
Combination ticket for adults (available only at Bowman's Hill and Tower) to historic buildings and the Tower, $3.00.

Brandywine Battlefield Park

On August 24, 1777 a British and Hessian army under Gen. William Howe, having sailed from New York and then up through Chesapeake Bay, landed at modern Elkton, Maryland. By September 10 it had marched northeastward and was concentrated near Kennett Square. The American army under George Washington had moved overland from the vicinity of New York City while the British were at sea, and was now deployed to cover the fords along Brandywine Creek, between the British and their apparent objective, Philadelphia.

Unknown to Washington, another ford — Jefferis' Ford — lay upstream from the most northerly of the crossings guarded by the Americans, but local Loyalists informed Howe of its existence. Early on the morning of September 11 the larger part of the British force, its movement hidden by fog, made a wide swing to the northwest to reach the ford undetected. Meanwhile, the remainder of Howe's army launched a diversionary attack against Washington's immediate front at Chadds Ford.

The Americans were completely deceived, believing the assault at Chadds Ford to be the main British attack. Nonetheless, when the flanking force hit them unexpectedly on their right, the troops in that sector succeeded in changing front to face their attackers. On the high ground around the Birmingham Meeting House they put up a determined fight, beating off repeated assaults until finally outflanked.

In the meantime, the Americans at Chadds Ford, faced now with a genuine attack instead of a mere demonstration, carried out an effective delaying action. Eventually they were forced into a withdrawal but, while it was a retreat, it was by no means a rout. The British held the ground when the battle

The battle, painted by F. C. Yohn

Lafayette's headquarters

ended, but they had won it at such a price that they were in no condition to mount a pursuit.

Although the Battle of Brandywine was a tactical defeat for the Americans, it had repercussions of the greatest importance. It was followed by the near-victory at Germantown on October 4 and by the spectacular victory on the Hudson leading to Gen. John Burgoyne's surrender of his invading army at Saratoga, New York on October 17. Thus, Brandywine launched a rapid succession of military events which indicated that an eventual American victory was a realistic possibility. France was eager to seize any promising opportunity to embarrass her hereditary enemy. Brandywine and the events which soon followed it gave reason to believe that the French Crown could lend support to the American rebels without the probability of wedding itself to a hopeless cause.

To explain the Battle of Brandywine, the Visitors Center contains orientation exhibits which include a slide presentation, two dioramas, weapons, and equipment. A museum store offers publications and other materials relating to Pennsylvania history, the Revolution and the battle. The house used by Washington as headquarters and the house where the young Marquis de Lafayette was quartered, both furnished in period style, are also open to visitors. The Birmingham Meeting House, around which some of the fiercest combat took place and which both armies used to care for their wounded, is still in use by the Society of Friends, but it may be viewed from the outside.

Regularly scheduled events include a re-enactment of Washington's arrival at his headquarters, presented annually on February 22; an encampment and equipment demonstrations by re-enactment units, held on the weekend before Memorial Day; and a Militia Muster Day, with an encampment, drill and tactical demonstrations by re-enactment units, conducted on the weekend closest to the anniversary of the battle (September 11)

Administered by: Pennsylvania Historical and Museum Commission, in cooperation with the Brandywine Battlefield Park Commission

Address: Brandywine Battlefield Park
Box 202
Chadds Ford, PA 19317
Telephone: (215) 459-3342

Location: U.S. Route 1, Chadds Ford, PA

Visiting hours: Tuesdays through Saturdays, 9 A.M.-5 P.M.
Sundays, 12 NOON-5 P.M. (Closed Mondays and State holidays)

Admission charge (includes admission to the Visitors Center, Washington's Headquarters, and Lafayette's Quarters):
Adults, $1.00
Youth (ages 6-17), $.50
Senior citizens and (by appointment) members of scheduled groups, $.75

Cliveden and the Battle of Germantown

Although a detachment of British troops occupied Philadelphia on September 26, 1777, Gen. William Howe was concerned about the possibility of an American attack from northwest of the city. Accordingly, he posted the major part of his army at Germantown in a line extending northeastward from just below the point where Wissahickon Creek flows into the Schuylkill, with a battalion manning a forward outpost at Mount Airy about a mile and a half to the north. Approximately halfway between, near a handsome house named Cliveden, was another battalion as back-up. Cliveden, which was empty, was the summer residence of Benjamin Chew, the Royal Chief Justice of Pennsylvania, who was currently in American custody as a suspected Loyalist.

Howe's suspicions were justified, for early on the morning of October 4 Washington launched an assault. His plan, overly elaborate, had four elements. The main attack was to be a frontal drive against the center of the British line. At the same time, another force was sent to strike the British northern (right) flank, and a third, moving along the Schuylkill, was to fall simultaneously on the British left flank. Still another column, marching behind the right-flank attack force, was to continue until it could swing down behind the British, cutting them off from Philadelphia.

The American advance was concealed by fog. The main attack swept the outpost and its back-up aside, then continued forward to strike the British line. The outpost, however, retreated only as far as Cliveden, where it took cover and began sniping at the Americans moving up to reinforce the main attack. On the advice of Gen. Henry Knox, Washington decided that he could not bypass such a threatening strongpoint, so he directed his reserve brigade to storm the house. Field pieces were brought forward to bombard it, but Cliveden's stone walls were proof against such lightweight cannon balls. Infantry charges were scythed down by British musket fire, and the few men who survived to reach the house were bayoneted as they tried to break in through the doors and windows. Finally, volunteers rushed forward with burning straw to set the house on fire, but all were shot down before coming close enough to accomplish their mission.

Meanwhile, the American flanking force to the north lost its way in the fog, reaching the battle zone to the left rear of the American forward line instead of on the British flank. In the fog this force mistook the Americans to its front for British and opened fire. Those troops, fired on from the left and hearing the noise of the fight at Cliveden to their rear, thought that they were surrounded and began a retreat which

Attack on Chew house, painted by Howard Pyle

spread all along the American line. This left the column moving down the Schuylkill with its left flank in the air, so it also withdrew without becoming engaged. The other column on the north, which was intended to envelop the British line, also got lost and never reached the battlefield. Washington's plan having disintegrated, he ordered a general withdrawal.

Thus, what had begun with such promise ended in failure. All the same, the British line had been on the verge of being broken. This near-success not only threw a genuine scare into General Howe but also, coming on the heels of the Battle of Brandywine and followed within days by the American successes on the Hudson ending in Gen. John Burgoyne's surrender at Saratoga, was clearly a symptom of American potential and British vulnerability, and therefore was to constitute an important factor in the French decision to enter the war on America's side.

Cliveden, which remained in the hands of the Chew family until 1972, is an eighteenth-century Georgian summer home located in a six-acre park in the center of Germantown, which is now within the city limits of Philadelphia. Pockmarks on the exterior walls and bullet holes in the interior woodwork provide mementos of the desperate battle waged there. Paintings of aspects of the engagement and an exhibit featuring muskets and other weapons of the period also commemorate the Battle of Germantown. While principal emphasis in the conducted tours is placed on the architectural style of the house and on its furnishings, which are original, a special tour for school groups which is available on request is devoted to the battle. Also, annually on the first Saturday of October, Revolutionary War re-enactment groups restage the fight for Cliveden and offer living history displays of soldier life, uniforms and equipment of the period.

A gift shop is operated in the house, offering for sale relevant publications, gifts pertinent to the period, and reproduction pieces from the collections of the National Trust for Historic Preservation.

Cliveden

Administered by: Cliveden, Inc., in co-stewardship with the National Trust for Historic Preservation
Address: Cliveden, Inc.
　　　　　6401 Germantown Ave.
　　　　　Philadelphia, PA 19144
　　　　　Telephone: (215) 848-1777
Location: 6401 Germantown Ave., Philadelphia, PA
Visiting hours: Tuesdays through Saturdays, 10 A.M.-4 P.M.
　　　　　Sundays 1-4 P.M. (Closed Mondays and major holidays)
Admission charge: Adults, $2.00
　　　　　Students, $1.00
　　　　　Senior citizens and members of tour groups, $1.50
　　　　　Members of the National Trust and of the Friends of Cliveden, None

Valley Forge National Historical Park and Valley Forge Historical Society Museum

The approach of the winter of 1777-1778 found the American army under George Washington occupying a line of hills at Whitemarsh, a few miles north of British-occupied Philadelphia. The area was strong defensively, but it was unsuitable for winter quarters and was too close to the British for safety. What was needed was a location near enough to Philadelphia to prevent the British from extending their control, but too far away for a sudden attack to achieve surprise. The place chosen was Valley Forge, eighteen miles west.

By dusk of December 19 the Americans completed the march to their new campsite. The first tasks were to make the position defensible and to erect shelters, so while some of the troops dug earthworks and installed obstacles, others were building huts. Both tasks were hampered by bad weather, the near nakedness of many of the men, acute shortages of food, and the rapid spread of sickness, but both were eventually accomplished. Although the winter did not prove to be especially severe, for almost three months the troops suffered great hardships.

However, winter quarters traditionally represented hardship. What gave Valley Forge its special importance was the arrival late in February of a Prussian volunteer, Friedrich von Steuben, who was assigned the task of developing and supervising a comprehensive training program. It must be remembered that most of the men at Valley Forge had been in the army for less than a year, and that during that time had been so occupied in maneuvering and fighting that there had been no opportunity for even the most rudimentary training. Through the late winter and into the spring, as conditions eased, the men were taught the basic skills of a soldier and indoctrinated with something they had never had — an understanding and sense of discipline. In particular, Steuben developed in the officers the concept of a chain of command and of the responsibility of each level of authority for those under its command. The result was that when the troops marched out of the camp on

Courtesy Valley Forge Historical Society

Washington reviews the troops, by William T. Trego

June 19, 1778 they constituted a responsive, disciplined, competent army. Its new effectiveness was promptly demonstrated under difficult circumstances at the Battle of Monmouth, fought on June 28.

Over the years, Valley Forge has come to be a symbol of the endurance and devotion of the men who won independence for the United States, and esteemed as one of the nation's most revered patriotic shrines. Here, in addition to a number of statues and monuments to individuals and organizations, the visitor can see reconstructions of the huts which housed the soldiers, rebuilt according to the specifications laid down in orders issued by Washington on arriving at the camp. Several of the redoubts, defensive obstacles, utility buildings, and headquarters guard huts have also been reconstructed. Open to visitors are the house rented by Washington for his

Carillon and Society museum

Re-created soldiers' huts

26

headquarters and residence, the lower floor representing an office and working area and the upper floor a living area, both furnished as they might have been at the time; the David Stevens House, where Gen. James Varnum of Rhode Island maintained his headquarters; and the Steuben Memorial Information Center, which has one room displaying period furniture and another devoted to memorabilia relating to Steuben and includes a set of panels illustrating movements of the drill he developed and taught to the troops.

The Park Visitors Center displays the marquee (large tent) used by Washington when he first arrived at Valley Forge. Also on display is an array of Revolutionary War weapons and equipment from the George C. Neuman collection. A museum shop offers a wide selection of books, pictures, posters, postcards, slides, and other materials dealing with the encampment, the Revolutionary War, George Washington and the park. (A commercially operated gift shop selling souvenirs is located beside Washington's Headquarters.)

Administratively independent of but physically adjacent to the Park is the museum of the Valley Forge Historical Society. One portion of the museum displays materials related to the encampment (including Washington's headquarters flag) and illustrating the growth of Valley Forge as a symbol. The other portion is devoted to memorabilia of George Washington, offering a collection that is exceeded only by the collections at the Smithsonian Institution and at Mount Vernon. The museum also includes a shop.

Events of particular interest at the Park are the re-enactment annually on December 19 of the entry of the troops into Valley Forge; the living history ex-

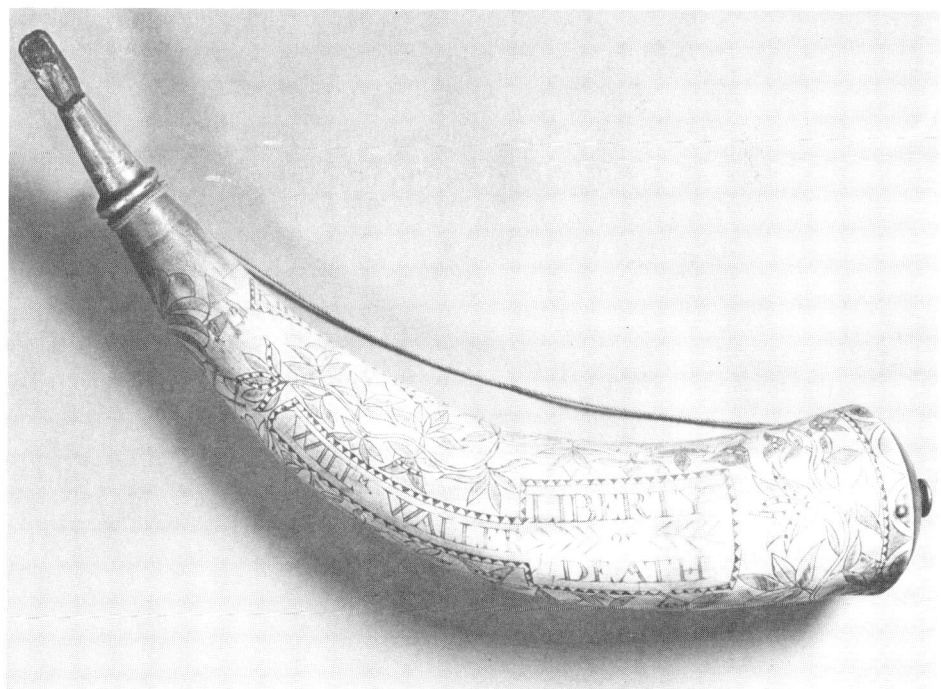

Courtesy Valley Forge Historical Society

Powder horn

hibit by the Muhlenberg Brigade, a reenactment unit, demonstrating period clothing, equipment and soldier life; an afternoon lecture on George Washington presented every year on the Monday nearest to February 22; and a continuing series of special programs.

The Park maintains an extensive library of works dealing with the Revolution, Washington, and the Valley Forge encampment, which may be used by researchers on Mondays and Wednesdays from noon until 4 P.M. The Valley Forge Historical Society also maintains a library, consisting of over seven hundred volumes devoted to Washington, which may be used by researchers by special appointment.

	Valley Forge National Historical Park	**Valley Forge Historical Society Museum**
Administered by:	National Park Service U.S. Department of the Interior	Valley Forge Historical Society
Address:	Valley Forge National Historical Park Valley Forge, PA 19481 Telephone: (215) 783-7700	Valley Forge Historical Society Box 122 Valley Forge, PA 19481 Telephone: (215) 783-0535
Location:	On Pa. 23, Valley Forge, PA	
Visiting hours:	Memorial Day through Labor Day Daily, 8:30 A.M.-6 P.M. Visitors Center Washington's Headquarters Daily, 9:30 A.M.-5 P.M. Varnum's House Steuben Memorial Information Center Muhlenberg Brigade Demonstrations Day after Labor Day to Memorial Day Daily, 8:30 A.M.-5 P.M. Visitors Center Washington's Headquarters Saturdays and Sundays 9:30 A.M.-5 P.M. Varnum's House 10 A.M.-4:30 P.M. Muhlenberg Brigade Demonstrations (Information on special programs can be obtained by telephone)	Monday through Saturdays, 9:30 A.M.-4:30 P.M. Sundays, 1-4:30 P.M. (Closed Christmas Day)
Admission charge:	None	$1 donation (Children under 10, none)

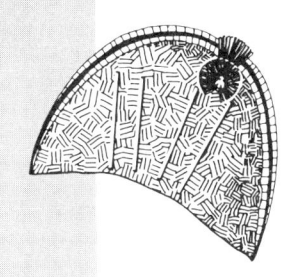

Section III
From the Revolution to 1812

ESTABLISHMENT of independence did not mean the end of military challenges. Although the Continental Navy and Marine Corps and all of the Continental Army except one company of artillery (half of it stationed at Fort Pitt) were disbanded by 1783, the Indian threat in the Old Northwest remained. Almost immediately, a standing force of militia was raised, most of it from Pennsylvania, to serve the national government under the Articles of Confederation. This force had been enlisted for only one year, but necessity led to its annual extension until ratification of the federal Constitution in 1789 provided the legal basis for embodying it in a regular army under the federal government.

Troubles abroad, initially with the Barbary pirates and later with France, soon brought the Navy and Marine Corps back into existence, and from time to time led to mobilizations of militia.

In all these events, Pennsylvania played a part, not only in the west but also on the coast, with Philadelphia serving as a naval base from which American sailors and marines put forth to protect the interests of the United States abroad and at sea.

Army-Navy Museum and Marine Corps Memorial Museum

Both these museums focus on the period from the Revolutionary War to approximately 1800.

The Army-Navy Museum offers an orientation film on the early history of these two services. Models illustrate uniforms of the period; back-lit pictures and maps explain major battles of the Revolutionary War; and weapons, equipment and other military artifacts are on exhibit. Of particular interest is the room fitted out as the lower-deck area of a naval vessel of the period, with gratings, cannon and the other features in the midst of which the sailors of that day lived, worked and fought.

The Marine Corps Memorial Museum has a diorama illustrating the Tun Tavern in Philadelphia, where the first Continental Marines were recruited. Also on display are a full-size mannequin in the Marine Corps uniform of the Revolutionary period, a cutaway scale model of an eighteenth-century warship, and a collection of paintings of Marine Corps campaigns of the era by Lt. Col. Charles Waterhouse.

New Hall (Marine Corps Memorial Museum)

Administered by: National Park Service, U.S. Department of the Interior

Address: Independence National Historical Park
 313 Walnut Street
 Philadelphia, PA 19106
 Telephone: (215) 597-8787

Location: Pemberton House (Army-Navy Museum)
 New Hall (Marine Corps Memorial Museum)
 (Both museums comprise part of the Independence National Historical Park)

Visiting hours: Daily, 9 A.M.-5 P.M. (Closed Christmas and New Year's days)

Admission charge: None

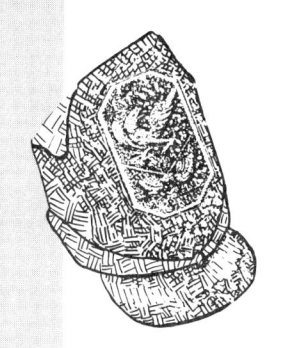

Section IV

The War of 1812 and Pennsylvania

PENNSYLVANIA'S chief involvement in the War of 1812 took the form of providing troops for service in other areas. However, Pennsylvania furnished the base as well as a number of the men for one of the most critical episodes of the war, the Battle of Lake Erie.

War with Britain was officially declared on June 19, 1812. By August, two thousand Pennsylvania militiamen had been assembled to join the American force at Buffalo, New York to attack Fort Erie, across the Niagara River. Although this operation was abandoned and the militia tours expired, another two thousand Pennsylvania militiamen soon joined the colors. Early in 1813 they moved into Ohio and helped build Fort Meigs on the Maumee River, a few miles inland from the point where it flows into Lake Erie. Their tours expired on April 2, but they voluntarily remained on duty for two more weeks until replacements from Kentucky could arrive. By so doing, they helped complete Fort Meigs, which consequently was able to withstand a four-day British siege which began soon after the Pennsylvanians left.

At the other end of the Commonwealth, British naval raids along the east coast posed a potential threat to Philadelphia. To meet this until Regular Army troops could be brought in, Pennsylvania militia units garrisoned Fort Mifflin, the stronghold which had served so well in defending the water approach to the city during the Revolution.

Later in the year, the center of attention once more shifted to the northwest. Commodore Oliver Hazard Perry was building a fleet at Erie to challenge British naval control of the lake. Its southern shore not only presented an exposed flank, but the lake also was a major link in a water route leading into the American heartland. Vulnerable as Perry's boatyards were, they were an open invitation to naval attack. To guard against this possibility, some fifteen hundred militiamen from Pennsylvania built and manned batteries protecting the harbor mouth. When Perry's fleet sailed to meet the British, a substantial number of the militiamen were aboard — some serving as seamen and others as marines — and took part in the decisive victory on September 10. This engagement, the Battle of Lake Erie, was the turning point in the war in the northeastern United States.

In 1814, Pennsylvanians joined Regular troops to sail across Lake Erie and destroy Port Dover in Canada. Others were with the American force which crossed the Niagara River to fight and win the Battle of Chippewa on July 5.

On the other front, however, success seemed to be favoring the British. On August 21 landing forces captured and burned Washington, D.C., and others captured Alexandria, Virginia a

Courtesy Pennsylvania Academy of the Fine Arts

The battle, painted by Thomas Birch

week later. They then returned to their ships, which sailed by way of the Chesapeake Bay to attack Baltimore.

Their approach raised fears that Pennsylvania itself might be invaded. That threat brought a major mobilization of the militia. Companies from sixteen counties quickly assembled. Some ten thousand men were posted at Marcus Hook and Kennett Square to guard Philadelphia, and another five thousand marched to York to meet any British overland movement from Baltimore. To help defend that city against the imminent threat, three Pennsylvania militia companies were rushed to join the Maryland regiments at North Point and took part in the battle there, which, on September 12-13, repulsed the British attack by land.

Having failed to outflank Fort McHenry in Baltimore harbor and unable to reduce it by a naval bombardment, the British amphibious force abandoned the effort and on September 14 set sail and departed.

That action marked the end of combat on the east coast and, for Pennsylvania, it essentially ended the war. The politically controversial nature of the conflict had caused much of the country to provide half-hearted support — and in some cases outright resistance — to the national effort. Pennsylvania, by contrast, could take pride in having responded in full to every request the federal government had made of it, and in so doing to have provided more men to the war effort than any other state in the nation.

The Flagship Niagara

Largely at the initiative of Sailing Master Daniel Dobbins of the U.S. Navy, a Pennsylvanian who had years of experience sailing Lake Erie, a project to build a fleet at Erie was put into operation before the end of 1812. Qualified shipwrights and craftsmen were brought in from the coast and materials were gathered from widespread sources. As the months passed the fleet neared completion, but experienced seamen were in inadequate supply. To fill the gap, Pennsylvania militiamen who had been protecting the shipyard were pressed into service and trained as far as possible for duty aboard ship. Even this expedient, however, left the force short-handed.

Finally, on August 12, 1813, the fleet of two brigs, six schooners, and a sloop was able to sail, with Oliver Hazard Perry's pennant as commodore flying from the brig *Lawrence*. For some weeks, resupplied through Dobbins' efforts, Perry kept station outside the harbor at Malden, Canada. He was unwilling to risk attacking in such a confined area, but was certain that in time the British squadron of two ships, two brigs, a schooner, and a sloop, under Capt. Robert Barclay, R.N., would have to come out to get provisions for the British army. On September 10 Perry's confidence was rewarded as Barclay's squadron put to sea.

Although the American vessels outnumbered the British, the two forces were at least equal in weight of metal — that is, the number and caliber of their cannon — though the guns of the British ships had greater range. Undaunted, Perry ordered his own vessel, the *Lawrence*, to close with the most manacing of the British craft, the *Queen Charlotte*, which was Captain Barclay's flagship. The captain of the American brig *Niagara* ignored Perry's orders to support him, so the *Lawrence* found herself fighting alone against the *Queen Charlotte*. The carnage was appalling. After a fight of more than two hours had inflicted extensive damage to the American ship and heavy casualties to her crew, Perry moved by rowboat to hoist his pennant on the *Niagara*, which under his direct orders now sailed forward into battle. Arriving as yet unscathed, she broke the British line of battle, and in efforts to escape, the *Queen Charlotte* ran foul of the British brig *Detroit*. Held dead in the water by each other, both these vessels struck their colors and the remaining craft of the British squadron quickly followed suit.

Oliver Hazard Perry

The consequences of this victory were far greater than the capture or destruction of the British squadron. Had the day ended differently, the British would have been in a position to dominate all the states along the Great Lakes, and the way would have been open to the interior of the American continent.

Reinforcements of British veterans from the campaigns against Napoleon in Europe were already en route; when they arrived, an offensive could have been mounted that, at the worst, might well have changed the entire course of United States development, and at the least would have extensively prolonged the war.

With the lake secure, the *Niagara* was anchored for some years at Misery Bay, near Erie. For a time, she served as a receiving ship to house naval personnel, but eventually was abandoned and allowed to sink. In 1913 she was raised and the process of restoration began, insuring the preservation of the vessel as a symbol of a heroic effort and a major victory.

Flagship *Niagara*

Aboard the *Niagara* today, reproduction cannon on the main deck represent the brig's primary armament. On the lower deck, visitors may see the crew's quarters. Periodically on certain Saturdays between May and August the "Ship's Company, U.S. Brig *Niagara*," a re-enactment group each of whose members assumes the identity of an actual member of the crew, acts out daily activities, demonstrating gun drill, conducting a ship's muster, and performing other regular duties. Living history demonstrations are also held regularly on Pennsylvania Charter Day (the Sunday nearest March 11), Perry Day (the Saturday nearest September 10), and William Penn Heritage Day (the Sunday nearest October 24). A flag-lowering ceremony is conducted on Flag Day (June 14).

Items and publications pertaining to Pennsylvania history, maritime history, the War of 1812, the Battle of Lake Erie, and the *Niagara* herself are for sale in the museum store, "The Shipwright."

Visitors to Erie who are interested in Pennsylvania's military heritage may also wish to tour the Anthony Wayne Blockhouse. This is a replica of the stronghold built on General Wayne's orders during the Indian wars of the 1790s, and is located on the grounds of the Pennsylvania Soldiers and Sailors Home.

Administered by: Pennsylvania Historical and Museum Commission in cooperation with the Flagship *Niagara* League

Address: Flagship *Niagara*
 80 State Street
 Erie, PA 16507
 Telephone: (814) 871-4596

Location: 80 State Street, Erie, PA

Visiting hours: Tuesdays through Saturdays, 9 A.M.-5 P.M.
 Sundays, 12 NOON-5 P.M. (Closed Mondays and State holidays, except Memorial, Independence, and Labor days)

Admission charge: Adults, $2.00
 Youth (ages 6-17), $1.00
 Senior citizens (aged 65 and over) and members of group tours, $1.50

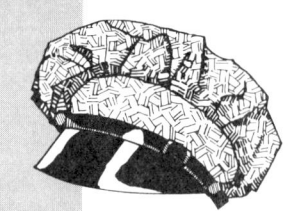

Section V
Pennsylvania and the Mexican War

LIKE the War of 1812, the war with Mexico, which was declared on May 13, 1846, was unpopular throughout much of the country. Also like the War of 1812, however, Pennsylvania gave enthusiastic support to the national effort. At the first call for troops, no less than ninety-eight companies of the Commonwealth's Volunteer Militia offered their services.

As it turned out, the federal government did not see a need for so many men, and in the end only two regiments, numbering twenty companies and designated the 1st and 2d Pennsylvania Volunteers, were mustered for active duty. In contrast to many of the other Volunteers, however, they were enlisted for two years' service rather than one.

After assembling at Pittsburgh, the two regiments moved by steamboat down the Ohio and Mississippi to arrive at New Orleans before the end of January 1847. From there they sailed with Gen. Winfield Scott's army to lay siege to the Mexican port of Vera Cruz, which was captured on March 29. The Americans then marched northwestward, with Mexico City as their final objective. They met their first obstacle at a fortified pass, Cerro Gordo, on April 18, with both Pennsylvania regiments taking part in the battle which swept the defenders aside. Less than two weeks later, however, the one-year enlistments of many of the Volunteer units expired and they left for home. Scott had no choice but to hold in place with the Regular Army units and two-year Volunteer regiments (among them the Pennsylvanians) at Puebla, only halfway to his goal, until new recruits could arrive from the United States. Among the men to reach Mexico at that time were two more Pennsylvania companies. These were absorbed into the 2d Pennsylvania Regiment.

Not until early August was it possible to resume the advance. The 1st Pennsylvania was left behind to garrison Puebla while the 2d Pennsylvania moved with the main army. By the night of September 11 the Americans were within three miles of Mexico City. On September 13 the Pennsylvanians took part in the general attack, overrunning a succession of defensive lines, and by nightfall had seized and occupied the fortified Gareta de Belen. On September 14 the Mexicans surrendered the city.

No single museum in the Commonwealth is devoted to Pennsylvania's participation in the Mexican War. However, exhibits relating to individuals and items of equipment, uniform and weapons associated with Pennsylvania's share in the struggle are on display at the Pennsylvania Military Museum at Boalsburg and the Soldiers and Sailors Memorial at Pittsburgh.

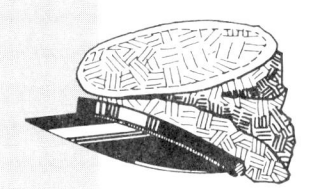

Section VI

The Civil War and Pennsylvania

ON APRIL 15, 1861, three days after Fort Sumter was fired on, President Lincoln issued a call to the governors of the northern states for seventy-five thousand Volunteers to serve for three months. Pennsylvania's response was the rapid mobilization of twenty-five regiments. Five Pennsylvania companies were the first Volunteers from the North to reach Washington, D.C., which was feared (groundlessly, it developed) to be threatened by immediate attack.

The three-month Volunteers saw only minor action, but many of them joined three-year regiments which began to be organized even before all the three-month men had been mustered out. Before the end of the war, Pennsylvania would raise more than two hundred regiments for the Union Army. While the bulk of these organizations served in the Army of the Potomac, fighting chiefly in Virginia, with a detour to Gettysburg in Pennsylvania, others operated along the Georgia and Carolina coast, and still others in the western theater — at Perryville, Stones River, Vicksburg, Chickamauga, Lookout Mountain, Missionary Ridge, in the Atlanta campaign, and in Sherman's march to Savannah. One Pennsylvania regiment was at the Battle of Shiloh, and another took part in the Red River campaign in Louisiana.

At times, Pennsylvania itself became the scene of combat. Aside from withstanding raids on border areas such as Chambersburg, one of the most crucial battles of American history, and one which has come to symbolize the Civil War as a whole, was fought at Gettysburg.

Participation of so many thousands of Pennsylvania's men and the especially significant involvement of its own territory have given the Civil War a particularly prominent place in the Commonwealth's military heritage. Testimony to that prominence is provided by the wealth of monuments and museums in the State devoted to commemoration of that great struggle.

State Archives and Museum Building

State Museum of Pennsylvania

In treating Pennsylvania's military history, the Pennsylvania Historical and Museum Commission addresses the different wars in a variety of museums in the statewide network it administers — the French and Indian War at Fort LeBoeuf, Fort Pitt and Bushy Run; the Revolutionary War at Washington Crossing, Brandywine and Fort Pitt; and the period from the latter nineteenth century to the present at the Pennsylvania Military Museum. At the Commission's central facility, however, the State Museum, the chief attention of the Military Gallery is to the Civil War.

The exhibit is organized thematically. One theme deals with the beginning of the war and centers around the five Pennsylvania companies, the "First Defenders," which were the first Volunteers from the North to reach Washington in April 1861 after President Lincoln's call for Volunteers. A second theme treats the role of Harrisburg, the State capital, in the war, with emphasis on Camp Curtin, one of the largest assembly and staging areas in terms of men processed through in any northern state. Another theme concentrates on the Battle of Gettysburg, a crucial turning point in the war. Pennsylvania's contribution to the war effort as a center of munitions manufacture is the subject of still a fifth series of exhibits. The presentation is rounded out by displays devoted to the details of soldier life in camp and in the field.

Military exhibits

The focal point of the exhibit is Peter F. Rothermel's heroic painting of the repulse of Pickett's Charge on July 3, 1863. Flanking it are two Civil War cannon, one of them a bronze "Napoleon," the workhorse gun of the field artillery of the period, and the other a steel "Griffen" six-pounder. On display are regimental colors, headquarters flags, and unit guidons of Pennsylvania organizations, and weapons, accoutrements, ammunition, drums and other equipment. Pictures of leading Pennsylvania military figures with uniforms and items of insignia they wore can be seen. A particularly fine component of the exhibit is the group of presentation swords and sabers, awarded to individual officers by their men or by citizens' groups in appreciation of their services.

Administered by: Pennsylvania Historical and Museum Commission
Address: State Museum of Pennsylvania
P.O. Box 1026
Harrisburg, PA 17108-1026
Telephone: (717) 787-4978
Location: North Third Street between North and Forster Streets, Harrisburg, PA
Visiting hours: Tuesday through Saturdays, 9 A.M.-5 P.M.
Sundays, 12 NOON-5 P.M. (Closed Mondays and State holidays)
Admission charge: None

The Civil War Library and Museum of the Military Order of the Loyal Legion of the United States

The Loyal Legion of the United States was founded as an organization of officers of the Union Army and is now made up of their descendants. The central library and museum for the national organization is located in Philadelphia, and presents the fruits of over a hundred years of collecting over the time since the museum was founded in 1886.

Portraits of leading figures of the Union Army and Navy adorn the walls. Entire rooms are devoted respectively to Gen. George Gordon Meade, a Pennsylvanian who commanded the Army of the Potomac from the Gettysburg campaign to the end of the war; to Gen. U. S. Grant, the Union Army's general-in-chief and later president of the United States; and to President Abraham Lincoln. Other rooms focus individually on memorabilia of the Confederate armed forces, among them three of the flags flown by the Confederate raider *Florida*; the United States Navy and documents, weapons and equipment of its enlisted men; and an armory of weapons, insignia and camp equipment. A period sitting room, fully furnished in the style of the time, commemorates the Dames of the Loyal Legion. Flags presented by the State government to Pennsylvania regiments are exhibited in the rotunda of the Capitol at Harrisburg, but most regiments also carried colors presented by the towns where the units were recruited, and a number of these are on display in the museum.

In addition to the wealth of artifacts and objects, the War Library has some twelve thousand books on the Civil War, along with several thousand original diaries, letters and other documents; a large collection of contemporaneous photographs; and a number of unpublished regimental histories in manuscript. With these are the archives of the Loyal Legion, which also represent valuable sources for researchers.

Administered by: Military Order of the Loyal Legion of the United States

Address: Military Order of the Loyal Legion of the United States
War Library and Museum
1805 Pine Street
Philadelphia, PA 19103
Telephone: (215) 735-8196

Location: 1805 Pine Street, Philadelphia, PA

Visiting hours: Mondays through Fridays, 10 A.M.-4 P.M.
(Open evenings and weekends by appointment)

Admission charge: Adults, $2.00
Organized educational groups and active-duty members of the U.S. Armed Forces, None

---

Soldiers and Sailors Memorial

The memorial to soldiers and sailors from Allegheny County who have served in American wars was dedicated in 1910, following almost two decades of planning initiated by the Allegheny County Grand Army Association, consisting of veterans of the Union Army and Navy.

Soldiers and Sailors Memorial

Understandably, the initial concentration was chiefly on the Civil War, and the memorabilia of that war form the largest part of the museum's collection. From the beginning, however, items pertaining to local units which fought in the Mexican War were included. As the years have passed, substantial quantities of equipment, uniform, weapons, captured materiel, and other items relating to America's subsequent conflicts and to the Marine Corps and Air Force have been added.

The Civil War collection includes portraits of prominent military figures from the county, sculptures, uniformed mannequins, paintings of battles on land and at sea, flags, items of personal equipment, regimental drums and military band instruments, medical instruments, and an entire array of weapons — swords and bayonets, rifles, pistols, cannon and ammunition. Bronze plaques mounted on the walls list the names, by organization, of the Allegheny County men who served in the Civil War. A portion of a tree trunk in which two cannon balls were embedded during the Battle of Chickamauga is a relic of special interest. Among tributes to individuals, a special display commemorates Mrs. Mary Leonard ("French Mary"), who was awarded the Kearny Cross for service as a vivandière with the 114th Pennsylvania Volunteers.

World War I exhibits include equipment such as mess kits and other personal items, trench weapons such as hand grenades and trench knives, and captured German materiel. Among the objects relating to more recent conflicts is the ship's bell from the cruiser U.S.S. *Pittsburgh* of World War II.

Addressing all the wars of the past century is the Hall of Valor, a meeting room whose walls bear the pictures and citations of all the men from Allegheny County who have been awarded America's highest decorations for heroism — the Medal of Honor, the Army's Distinguished Service Cross, the Navy Cross and the Air Force Cross. Represented here are conflicts ranging from the Civil War through the Philippine Insurrection, the Boxer Rebellion, the two World Wars, and the Korean and Vietnam wars.

For researchers, the library offers a wide collection of volumes, primarily on the Civil War, many of which are otherwise difficult to locate, along with regimental histories and muster rolls of units recruited in the area. Included in the collection are unpublished documents, letters, original copies of military communications, and the records of all Allegheny County posts of the Grand Army of the Republic.

Administered by: Soldiers and Sailors Memorial of Allegheny County

Address: Soldiers and Sailors Memorial of Allegheny County
Fifth and Bigelow
Pittsburgh, PA 15213
Telephone: (412) 621-4253

Location: Fifth and Bigelow, Pittsburgh, PA

Visiting hours: Mondays through Saturdays, 9 A.M.-4 P.M.
Sundays, 1-4 P.M.
(Closed New Year's, Labor, Thanksgiving, and Christmas days)

Admission charge: None

Gettysburg National Military Park

Gettysburg is the site of one of the most climactic events in American history. There, on July 1-3, 1863, Gen. George G. Meade's Army of the Potomac and Gen. Robert E. Lee's Confederate Army of Northern Virginia met in a combat which marked a major turning point in the course of the war. With ninety-seven thousand Federal troops and seventy-five thousand Confederates engaged, it was the largest battle ever fought on United States soil. With some fifty-one thousand casualties, it was one of the bloodiest.

In June 1863 the Confederates had moved north from Virginia, confident from their recent victory at Chancellorsville, with Harrisburg, Pennsylvania as their objective. Meade followed along a roughly parallel route. In each case, such large forces had to move along different routes, and the main elements of both armies were widely separated from each other when one part of the Confederate army, approaching Gettysburg from the northwest, unexpectedly encountered an element of the federal army coming up from the south.

The initial contact on July 1 was made on the western edge of the village. Each commander then hurried to rush reinforcements to the battlefield. For a time the Federals held a line along the north-south Seminary Ridge, but the arrival of a Confederate army corps coming south from Carlisle struck the right flank of the Federals, who retreated through the town to establish a new line anchored on another north-south elevation, southeast of town, called Cemetery Ridge. From that position they were able to beat back a major assault, and as reinforcements came up the line was extended southward.

On the next day Lee launched what was to be a coordinated assault on the federal right, center and left, intended to roll up the Federal line and crush it. Instead of striking simultaneously, however, the attacks were carried out one at a time, and Meade was able to rush reinforcements from one part of the field to another to meet each attack in turn. This day saw some of the bitterest fighting of the battle and imposed the highest single toll of casualties.

The climax came on July 3. After an artillery bombardment of a length and weight unprecedented in that war, Lee launched a massive assault ("Pickett's Charge") against the center of the Federal line. Although its forward edge almost broke through, it was finally shattered in fierce hand-to-hand fighting and the surviving Confederates fell back to Seminary Ridge.

The two armies kept a wary eye on each other through July 4, but on the following day Lee began a retreat to Virginia. The Federals followed, but they were too exhausted to mount a vigorous pursuit, so the Confederates were able to cross the Potomac into Virginia. The war would continue for almost two more years, but any real chance for a Confederate victory had been lost in 1863 on Cemetery Ridge at Gettysburg.

Today, Gettysburg stands as a patriotic shrine comparable to Valley Forge. Virtually the whole town is a monument, and buildings which existed at the time of the battle are marked with small bronze plaques. Giving the location a special poignancy is the presence of the National Cemetery, where many of the battle's dead lie buried, and at whose dedication President Lincoln delivered his immortal address.

The fields and wood lines remain much as they were in 1863, but in every direction are monuments, cannon and markers commemorating particular individuals, organizations and events of the struggle — with over three thou-

Battlefield scene

Pennsylvania Monument

sand monuments in the park, it has been said that Gettysburg is the most extensively marked battlefield in the world. A roadnet which connects the locations of key importance in the battle without violating the integrity of the site permits tours by automobile; guides licensed by the park authorities may be hired at the Visitors Center, and tape cassettes for self-guided tours may be rented from commercial sources in the town.

A point of particular interest is the Cyclorama Center. Its ground floor features exhibits of photographs and artworks relating to the Civil War in general and to the Battle of Gettysburg in particular. From April through Labor Day, one of the original copies of Lincoln's Gettysburg Address is displayed. A gift shop is maintained, primarily to offer Civil War books and other publications. On the upper floor is the Cyclorama itself, where a sound-and-light show explains the climax of the struggle by examining in sequence the several segments of the famous circular painting of Pickett's Charge by Paul Philippotaux.

The Visitors Center contains several important facilities. Its museum presents the Rosensteel Collection of Civil War artifacts and weapons, together with exhibits of uniform items, camp life, music, the navies of both contestants, duty and leisure-time activities of enlisted men, and the story of the battle and its effect on the town. The gift shop has for sale a wide assortment of publications on the war, the battle, and leading personalities, ranging from works intended for serious students to those appealing to the visitor having only a general interest in the subject. It also offers slides, postcards, records and tapes of Civil War music, and video cassettes of the park. Still a third feature is the widely renowned "electric map," a large terrain model which uses flashing lights and a taped narration to explain the entire sequence of events.

Throughout the town, outside the park itself, are numerous private, commercially operated museums and souvenir shops.

A special annual event is held during the first week of July. Named "Civil

43

War Heritage Days," it is a combined undertaking involving community groups and Gettysburg College as well as the National Battlefield Park. Among the activities featured are a Civil War encampment in the park and, at the college, a series of lectures on various aspects of the Civil War.

For researchers, the park maintains a collection of reference materials. Among these are some thirty-five hundred volumes, including such items as regimental histories and personal accounts of the battle which are long out of print; manuscript files primarily relating to the park and its development; and approximately twenty-two thousand photographs (including a number relating to the Eisenhower Farm).

The Eisenhower Farm, President Eisenhower's retirement home, is located nearby and is open to visitors.

Administered by: National Park Service, U.S. Department of the Interior
Address: Gettysburg National Military Park
Gettysburg, PA 17325
Telephone: (717) 334-1124
Location: Gettysburg, PA

	Visiting Hours:	**Admission Charge**
Visitors Center:	Summer (mid-June to Labor Day), 8 A.M.-6 P.M. Winter, 8 A.M.-6 P.M. (Closed New Year's, Thanksgiving, Christmas days)	Visitors Center and Museum: None Electric Map: Adults (aged 16 and over $1.50) Senior citizens (aged 62 and over), $1.00
Cyclorama Center:	Daily, 8:30 A.M.-5 P.M. (Closed New Years, Thanksgiving, Christmas days)	Museum: None Cyclorama: Adults (aged 16 and over), $1.00 Senior citizens (aged 62 and over, holding "Golden Eagle," "Golden Age," or "Golden Access" passports), None
Library:	Mondays through Fridays, 8 A.M.-5 P.M. (Closed federal holidays)	None

Section VII

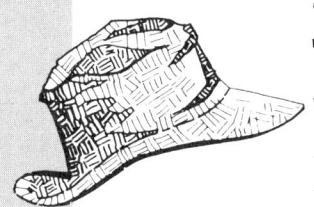

The Spanish-American War and the Philippine Insurrection

THE end of the Civil War brought to the United States a period of peace which lasted until 1898. On April 25 of that year, angered over the treatment of the Cubans by the Spaniards who exercised colonial control over the island and outraged when the battleship U.S.S. *Maine* was blown up in Havana harbor, the United States declared war on Spain.

In short order Pennsylvania mobilized its National Guard, providing thirteen infantry regiments along with cavalry and artillery for federal service. On May 1, while these units were still assembling, United States naval forces in the Far East, commanded by Commodore George Dewey, defeated the Spanish squadron in the Philippines at the Battle of Manila Bay. With the Philippine native population seizing the opportunity to throw off the control of their Spanish masters, American troops were sent to reinforce them. Among these troops, the only infantry regiment from the eastern part of the United States was the 10th Pennsylvania Infantry. On its arrival, it became the first American unit in the Philippines to engage in combat with the Spanish on land.

The campaign in Cuba proved to be of short duration, and none of the Pennsylvania Volunteer units reached the island. In the other campaign in that region, however, the invasion of Puerto Rico, the Pennsylvania cavalry and artillery units and the 4th and 16th Pennsylvania Infantry regiments were part of the landing force, although only the 16th Pennsylvania took part in the one brief action that occurred before hostilities were formally ended.

Across the world the situation was considerably different when the United States decided to establish control over the Philippines. The Spaniards surrendered Manila on August 13, but soon the Americans found themselves in combat with the Filipinos. After helping to beat off the Filipino attack that opened hostilities on February 4, 1899, the 10th Pennsylvania took part in the offensive campaign which ended on March 31 with the occupation of Malolos, the Filipinos' provisional capital. The regiment, substantially reduced by casualties and sickness, was withdrawn from active combat until July 1, when it was returned to the United States as part of the program releasing all state Volunteer units from active duty.

The services of Pennsylvanians in the Spanish-American War and the Philippine Insurrection are commemorated by the cruiser *Olympia*, Dewey's flagship at the Battle of Manila Bay, and at the Pennsylvania Military Museum by uniforms, weapons, and equipment of the war and by a diorama illustrating the charge of the 10th Pennsylvania Volunteers on La Loma Church at Manila, March 5, 1899.

The Cruiser Olympia

As the crisis in relations between the United States and Spain increased, directions on the action to be taken if war broke out were sent to Commodore George Dewey, commanding the Asiatic Squadron of the U.S. Navy. Two days after war was declared he sailed from Chinese waters for the Philippine Islands, Spain's nearest colonial outpost.

Dewey's squadron consisted of two gunboats and five cruisers. One of the cruisers, the *Olympia,* commanded by an adopted Pennsylvanian, Capt. Charles V. Gridley, served as Dewey's flagship. On the night of April 30 the *Olympia* led the squadron into Manila Bay, eluding the submarine mines and the harbor fortress of Corregidor. On the following day the Americans attacked. It was to the captain of the *Olympia* that Dewey issued his famous order, "You may fire when you are ready, Gridley," signaling the beginning of a bombardment which utterly destroyed the Spanish squadron anchored off the fortified naval yard at Cavite.

After the war the *Olympia* was for a time the flagship of the North American Squadron. During World War I, as flagship of the United States Patrol Force, she performed escort and patrol duty off New York and Nova Scotia, later transporting a force to Murmansk to maintain order after the Russian surrender to the Central Powers, and finally becoming the flagship of the U.S. Naval Forces Eastern Mediterranean. After the war the *Olympia* returned the

The *Olympia* and *Becuna*

body of the Unknown Soldier from France for burial in Arlington National Cemetery. This was her final assignment before being decommissioned.

In 1957 she was acquired on lease from the U.S. Navy by the Cruiser *Olympia* Association, which carried out extensive restorations. Visitors may follow self-conducted tours through the cruiser, viewing the officers' quarters, engine room, sickbay, crew quarters, admiral's cabin and stateroom, captain's cabin and stateroom, the galley, the spot where the casket of the Unknown Soldier lay, the flag office and signal office, the forward gun turret, and the pilot house, conning tower, and forward bridge.

Alongside lies a modified World War II submarine, the U.S.S. *Becuna*, which also may be toured. She contains a small museum of artifacts, battle charts, and uniforms relating to the submarine's service.

A "Ship's Store" sells a variety of souvenir items, including coins made from one of the *Olympia's* propellers. All proceeds are used to support maintenance costs.

Administered by: Cruiser *Olympia* Association

Address: Cruiser *Olympia* Association
P.O. Box 928
Philadelphia, PA 19105
Telephone: (215) 922-1898

Location: Delaware and Spruce Streets, Philadelphia, PA

Visiting hours: Winter (months of Standard Time), 10 A.M.-4:30 P.M.
Summer (months of Daylight Savings Time)
Mondays through Fridays, 10 A.M.-5 P.M.
Saturdays and Sundays, 10 A.M.-6 P.M.

Admission charge (includes both *Olympia* and *Becuna*):
Adults, $2.50
Children under age 12, $1.25
Senior citizens, $1.50
(Special group rates are available by prior arrangement)

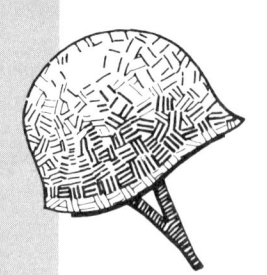

Section VIII
The Pennsylvania Military Museum

THE Pennsylvania Military Museum, dealing primarily with the history of the Pennsylvania National Guard after its inception following the Civil War, also devotes attention to the National Guard's forerunners back to the French and Indian War. Thus, while not treating Pennsylvania's entire military history in detail, its coverage transcends any one war. The special focus is on the conflicts from World War I to the present.

Sherman tank

Museum

The present museum originated with the 28th Division Shrine, administered initially by the Society of the 28th Division A.E.F. as a memorial to that organization's World War I service, on land donated by one of the division's veterans, Col. Theodore Boal. Following a period under the jurisdiction of the Pennsylvania Department of Military Affairs, the site was transferred in 1957 to the Pennsylvania Historical and Museum Commission.

Displayed on the grounds are artillery pieces, caissons and limbers, and a World War II Sherman tank. Exhibits in the museum itself trace the evolution of Pennsylvania's citizen-soldiers from the earliest times, providing background for the explanation of the creation of the National Guard in the 1870-1871 era. Mementos of Spanish-American War service include various accoutrements, individual equipment, and captured items, as well as a diorama of the 10th Pennsylvania's 1899 charge on La Loma Church in the Philippines.

A weapons room contains firearms from each war in which Pennsylvanians have participated. An exhibit of special interest is the full-size replica of a World War I trench system, complete with uniformed mannequins at their ready positions, which is given a further sense of realism by the sounds and flashes of gunfire. Nearby, as a grim reminder of the costs of battle, is a forward aid post and ambulance.

World War I ambulance crew

An entire gallery is devoted to the experience of Pennsylvania soldiers, sailors, airmen, and marines in World War II and during the Korean War. Clothing and equipment are accompanied by materials related to individuals of all ranks and services who played conspicuous roles in command and in combat. Finally, a display commemorates events of the Vietnam War.

Administered by: Pennsylvania Historical and Museum Commission

Address: Pennsylvania Military Museum
P.O. Box 148
Boalsburg, PA 16827
Telephone: (814) 466-6263

Location: Boalsburg, PA

Visiting hours: Tuesdays through Saturdays, 9 A.M.-5 P.M.
Sundays, 12 NOON-5 P.M. (Closed Mondays and State holidays except Memorial, Independence and Veterans days)

Admission charge: Adults: $1.50
Youths (ages 6-18), $1.50
Senior citizens (aged 65 and over), $1.00
(Special rates for groups can be arranged by prior appointment)

Section IX
Regimental Museum

ONE museum commemorating the service of an individual regiment of the Pennsylvania Army National Guard is treated separately because, while visits may be arranged by special appointment, it is not open to the public on a regularly scheduled basis.

Museum of the First Troop, Philadelphia City Cavalry

With an unbroken record of continuous service going back to 1774, the First Troop, Philadelphia City Cavalry is one of the oldest American military organizations to be still in existence, serving today as Troop A, 1st Squadron, 104th Cavalry, 28th Infantry Division. Its museum features an extensive collection of U.S. cavalry weapons — including examples of sabers, pistols, and all carbines ever issued to U.S. mounted troops — as well as cavalry accoutrements and uniforms from the colonial era to the present. Also included are trophies, portraits, silver, porcelain, sculpture and original documents associated with distinguished members of the Troop and with historic figures with whom it was associated, paintings depicting memorable events in which it took part, and photographs of its service. Of special interest among the flags and guidons which are on display is the Troop's original standard, dating from 1775, which is one of the few regimental colors surviving from the Revolutionary War.

Administered by: First Troop, Philadelphia City Cavalry

Address: The Armory
23rd and Rumstead Streets
Philadelphia, PA 19103
Telephone: (215) 654-1488

Visiting hours: Mondays through Fridays, 8:30 A.M.-4:30 P.M. (by appointment)

Admission charge: None